HELLO NEIGHBOR

CANADA

by Jeri Cipriano

Red Chair Press   Egremont, Massachusetts

Look! Books are produced and published by Red Chair Press:

Red Chair Press LLC   PO Box 333   South Egremont, MA 01258-0333

www.redchairpress.com

Publisher's Cataloging-In-Publication Data

Names: Cipriano, Jeri S.

Title: Canada / by Jeri Cipriano.

Description: Egremont, Massachusetts : Red Chair Press, [2019] | Series: Look! books : Hello neighbor | Interest age level: 004-008. | Includes index, Now You Know fact boxes, a glossary and resources for further reading. | Summary: "The United States and Canada share many things including the world's longest border between two countries. In this book, readers will discover many more things the two neighbors have in common as well as some of the differences that make each country unique."--Provided by publisher.

Identifiers: ISBN 9781634403276 (library hardcover) | ISBN 9781634403696 (paperback) | ISBN 9781634403320 (ebook)

Subjects: LCSH: Canada--Social life and customs--Juvenile literature. | Canada--Description and travel--Juvenile literature. | United States--Social life and customs--Juvenile literature. | United States--Description and travel--Juvenile literature. | CYAC: Canada--Social life and customs. | Canada--Description and travel. | United States--Social life and customs. | United States--Description and travel.

Classification: LCC F1008.2 .C56 2019 (print) | LCC F1008.2 (ebook) | DDC 971 [E]--dc23

LCCN: 2017963405

Photo credits: iStock except for the following; p. 12: Dinardo Design

Printed in the United States of America

0918 1P CGS19

Table of Contents

All About Canada

Hello and *Bonjour* (Bohn-zhur) from Canada. The United States and Canada are neighbors.

Good to Know

The **border** between Canada and the U.S. is the longest border in the world.

North Pacific Ocean

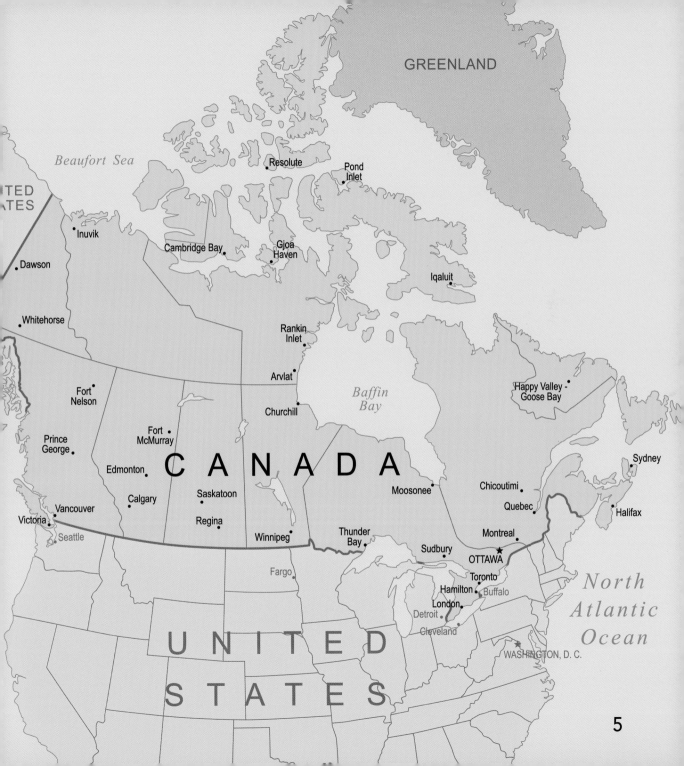

GREENLAND

Beaufort Sea

Resolute

Pond Inlet

ITED STATES

Inuvik

Dawson

Cambridge Bay

Gjoa Haven

Iqaluit

Whitehorse

Rankin Inlet

Arvlat

Baffin Bay

Happy Valley - Goose Bay

Fort Nelson

Churchill

Prince George

Fort McMurray

C A N A D A

Sydney

Edmonton

Moosonee

Chicoutimi

Calgary

Saskatoon

Quebec

Halifax

Victoria

Vancouver

Regina

Winnipeg

Thunder Bay

Montreal

Seattle

Sudbury

OTTAWA ★

Fargo

Toronto

Hamilton

Buffalo

North Atlantic Ocean

London

Detroit

Cleveland

U N I T E D

WASHINGTON, D. C.

S T A T E S

5

Canada's flag is red and white. It shows a maple leaf. The maple leaf is a **symbol** for strength. The bald eagle stands for strength in the U.S.

Good to Know

Today, Canada produces most of the world's maple syrup. That's a sweet fact!

6

The **capital** of Canada is Ottawa. A large **canal** runs through the city. Water in the canal freezes in winter and people skate on it.

Good to Know

In 2017, Canada celebrated its 150th Birthday!

Ice Hockey is Canada's most popular sport. Ice hockey was **invented** here in the 1850s. The Hockey Hall of Fame is in Toronto.

Good to Know

Canada has two languages: English and French. In a big city like Vancouver there are signs in both languages.

BIENVENUE
WELCOME TO
VANCOUVER
Host City - 2010 Olympic And Paralympic Winter Games
Ville hôte - Jeux olympiques et paralympiques d'hiver de

Canada's money looks different from U.S. money, but the names are the same. Canada has a coin that glows in the dark. Would you spend it or save it?

Good to Know

Canada's paper money has markings so blind people can "read" the bills and tell them apart.

The Land and People

Canada is the second largest country in the world. A big part of it is inside the **Arctic Circle**. The land here is frozen ten months of the year. Polar bears live in this part of Canada.

Good to Know

Every year, icebergs from Greenland float to Canada. Visitors come from all around to see the icebergs before they melt.

First Nation People

Canada is home to First Nation people. These people have lived in Canada for thousands of years. That was long before explorers from Europe arrived.

The Inuit are **native** people from the Arctic area.

Animals

Atlantic Puffin

The puffin can catch up to ten fish with just one dive underwater.

Caribou

If there is danger, these animals stand on their back legs. They are often called reindeer.

Good to Know

Winnie-the-Pooh was based on a real bear cub from Winnipeg, Manitoba in Canada.

Celebrations

Winter Festivals are held across the country. The biggest is Winter Carnival or Carnaval de Québec in Quebec City. You can race canoes on ice, play ice hockey, and build snow art.

July 1 is <u>Canada Day</u>. This is the day in 1867 that three colonies united to become one in the British Empire.

Teams race canoes on ice in Québec.

Words to Keep

Arctic Circle: the area at the north pole of Earth

border: the land separating two countries

canal: a human-made waterway

capital: city where a nation's government is based

invented: was first played

native: someone or something that was the first in a place.

symbol: something that represents or stands for something else.

Learn More at the Library

Books (Check out these books to learn more.)

Juarez, Christine. *Canada*. Capstone Press, 2014.

McDonnell, Ginger. *Next Stop: Canada*. Teacher Created Materials, 2011.

Parkes, Elle. *Let's Explore Canada* (Bumba Books). Lerner Publishing, 2018.

Web Sites (Ask an adult to show you this web site.)

Kids' World Travel Guide
www.kids-world-travel-guide.com/canada-facts-for-kids.html

Index

About the Author

Jeri Cipriano has written and edited many books for young readers. She likes making new friends from different places. Jeri lives and writes in New York state.